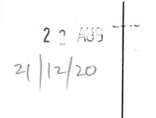
Henry Brook

Designed by Anna Gould, Helen Edmonds and Will Dawes

Illustrated by Staz Johnson, Adrian Roots and Ian McNee

Edited by Alex Frith

Survival exper

Contents

Adventurers must swim across pools, rope down sheer cliffs and jump across gaps to reach the foot of Claustral Canyon, part of the Blue Mountain region in New South Wales, Australia.

Staying alive

Survival is about overcoming challenges and living to see another day. Some challenges come about entirely by accident. More often, the greatest feats of survival are accomplished by adventurers, explorers and daredevils.

The force of nature

Survival skills help people cope with all sorts of natural hazards, from earthquakes to wild storms or animal attacks. Key skills in these unpredictable situations include careful decision making and the ability to keep calm under pressure.

Hurricane force winds batter the town of Puerto San Carlos, Mexico.

To the ends of the Earth

With the right clothing, equipment and training, humans can adapt and survive anywhere, from parched deserts to icy caves and even stormy seas.

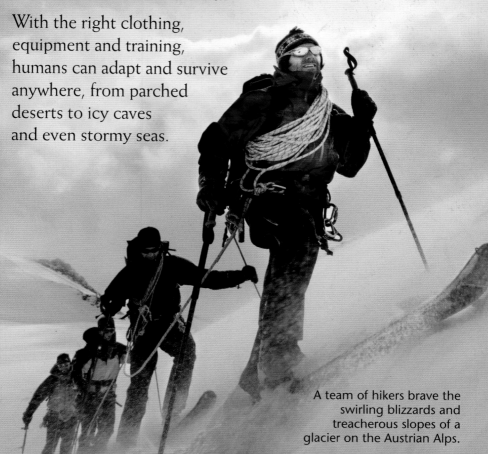

A team of hikers brave the swirling blizzards and treacherous slopes of a glacier on the Austrian Alps.

Survival zones	
• **Deserts** bake with heat during the day, but can be freezing cold at night. Find out more on pages 16-17. • **Tropical jungles** combine searing heat with bursts of heavy rain, and the constant threat of animal attacks and insect bites. Find out more on pages 48-49.	• **Mountain peaks**, along with the Arctic and Antarctic regions, are bitterly cold and hide treacherous cracks. Find out more on pages 26-27. • **The open ocean** is the biggest wilderness on Earth, with its own set of dangers. Find out more on pages 56-57.

The will to live

Most survival stories end with a person or team being rescued. The people most likely to make it through are those who cling to life at all costs, and who know how to improve their chances of being found.

1. Lost in the jungle

What do you do if you find yourself alone in the middle of a jungle?

Survival priorities:

- Find water and food
- Find a way out
- Guard against insects and other animals

On page 50, find out how a young German tourist survived a jungle ordeal for 9 days.

2. Plane crash in the desert

Surviving a crash landing is one thing, but the real challenge is escaping from the barren emptiness of a vast desert.

Survival priorities:

- Find water
- Build shelter during the day
- Attract attention

On page 18, find out how two French adventurers coped.

3. Grizzly bear attack

Grizzly bears are among the most dangerous animals on land.

Survival priorities:

• Get medical help

On page 40, find out how an American fur trapper coped after being mauled by a grizzly.

4. Adrift at sea

If you need to abandon ship in the open ocean, a liferaft will help keep you safe, but may not be able to get you to land.

Survival priorities:

• Attract the attention of rescuers
• Find food and water
• Guard against the Sun

On page 60, find out how a couple survived for 117 days in the open ocean.

5. Trapped in the ice

Explorers to the Arctic and Antarctic always set off well-prepared, but in a barren land of ice, supplies can't last forever...

Survival priorities:

• Head in the right direction
• Watch out for sea ice
• Detect and avoid crevasses

On page 28, find out how a team of explorers escaped from the remote continent of Antarctica.

Snow goggles

This climber has an ice tool in each hand, to dig into and grip on the ice.

Suiting up

The right equipment, coupled with the right training to use it, can make the difference between life and death. Here's what experts carry:

Mountains and Arctic zones

- Up to seven layers of clothing to trap warmth and guard against wind chill
- Spikes called *crampons* can be fixed to boots to provide a sturdy grip on snow and ice.

Crampons

Tropical zones

- Machete blade to hack through thick jungle branches
- Thick socks up to the knees to protect against leeches and other biting creatures

Desert zones

- Goggles to guard against sand storms
- Head scarf to shield head and neck against sunlight
- Lightweight backpack filled with water

Know your limits

Time is precious in all survival situations.

Three minutes

It's very hard to hold your breath for more than *three minutes*. Being able to breathe clean air is always the top priority.

Three hours

Cold, damp conditions can leave a person helpless in just *three hours*. Get out of the cold and the rain, and – in many deserts – the searing heat.

Three days

Thirst can kill in *three days*. Only drink clean, ideally freshly boiled, water. Drinking contaminated or salty water can make a bad situation worse.

Three weeks

Extreme hunger leaves a person too weak to move, and can kill in *three weeks*. Even a small store of food will give a survivor energy for several days.

Tool kit

Some pieces of equipment can help in almost any situation, even in the harshest climates on Earth.

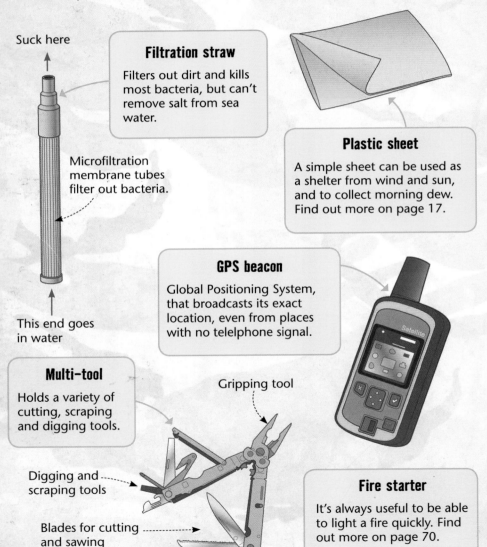

Suck here

Filtration straw

Filters out dirt and kills most bacteria, but can't remove salt from sea water.

Microfiltration membrane tubes filter out bacteria.

This end goes in water

Plastic sheet

A simple sheet can be used as a shelter from wind and sun, and to collect morning dew. Find out more on page 17.

GPS beacon

Global Positioning System, that broadcasts its exact location, even from places with no telephone signal.

Satellite

Multi-tool

Holds a variety of cutting, scraping and digging tools.

Gripping tool

Digging and scraping tools

Blades for cutting and sawing

Fire starter

It's always useful to be able to light a fire quickly. Find out more on page 70.

Solar light

Solar-powered lights charge up during daylight.

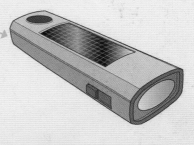

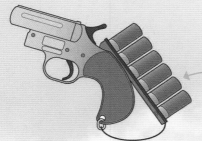

Flare gun pistol

Shoots light or smoke signals, called *flares*, into the air.

A wilderness rescue helicopter is drawn to the smoke of a distress flare in the Scottish Highlands.

Once in sight, it's best to angle the flare away from the helicopter to avoid clouding the pilot's view.

On the rock face

Mountaineering calls for specialized equipment to provide maximum safety and even comfort.

1 Solar charging blanket provides power for battery-operated kit.

2 Rubber sheets for extra insulation

3 Carabiners or Karabiners – hooks for ropes

4 Sleeping bag; can keep a person warm in temperatures as low as -50°C (-60°F)

5 Portaledge tent

6 Climbing boots

7 Water filter

8 Climbing ropes

Safe as houses

Some climbers carry a two-person sleeping platform called a *portaledge* that anchors to any rock face. This climber is in Yosemite National Park, USA.

The Namib Desert stretches along the west coast of Southern Africa. Water is incredibly scarce – grasses and beetles only survive by absorbing fog that rolls in from the ocean.

Survival zone:
Deserts

The world's desert regions are full of dangers, with burning heat in the daytime and temperatures close to freezing at night.

Deserts are dry places that get very little rain. Some are sandy; others dry and dusty. None are easy for plants and animals to survive in.

Animal hazard: rattlesnakes

- **Longest:** Eastern diamondback – 2.5m (8ft)
- **Deadliest venom:** Mojave rattlesnake
- **Death toll on humans:** less than 10 per year
- **Main location:** deserts of North and South America

Blowing hot and cold

If you break down in the desert, always stay with your vehicle. It provides shelter and shade and you have a better chance of being spotted by rescuers.

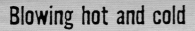

Finding water

- Look for any sign of vegetation.
- Follow trails of insects, or flocks of birds.
- Look for low land, such as a valley carved out by an old, dried-up river, and dig down a few feet.

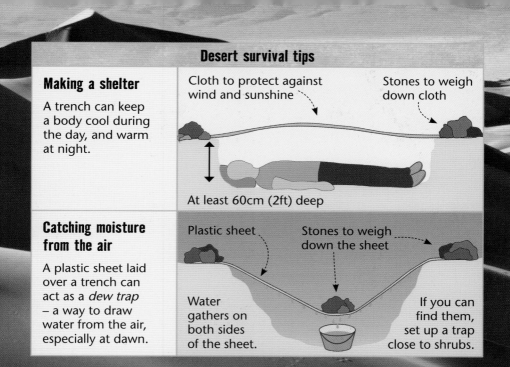

Desert survival tips

Making a shelter

A trench can keep a body cool during the day, and warm at night.

Cloth to protect against wind and sunshine

Stones to weigh down cloth

At least 60cm (2ft) deep

Catching moisture from the air

A plastic sheet laid over a trench can act as a *dew trap* – a way to draw water from the air, especially at dawn.

Plastic sheet

Stones to weigh down the sheet

Water gathers on both sides of the sheet.

If you can find them, set up a trap close to shrubs.

This is Death Valley in California, USA. This part of the world holds the world record for the hottest air temperature: 56°C (134°F). In winter, the temperature can fall as low as -7°C (19°F) at night.

Lost in the desert

DATE: December, 1935

LOCATION: The Sahara Desert, in North Africa.

BACKGROUND: French aviators Antoine de Saint-Exupéry and André Prévot were attempting to win an air speed race from Paris to the Far East.

Disaster strikes

In the night skies over north Africa, the pair found themselves lost in a cloud and running low on fuel. Drifting off route, they crashed into a desert plateau...

...but both emerged from the wreck without a scratch. They spent the rest of the night in the broken plane.

Day 1. The pair walked for 32km (20 miles), finding nothing but sand and rock. They retreated to the safety of the wreckage.

Day 2. Saint-Exupéry walked alone, heading in a different direction. He imagined seeing towns and lakes, but they were mirages – tricks of the eye.

Prevot lit a fire, hoping the smoke would draw attention. Nobody came.

Desperate for water, the pair stretched out a parachute over a shallow pit.

In the morning, they drank dew that collected on the underside of the silk.

Day 3. Giving up hope of rescue, both men left the plane, and covered 80km (50 miles).

They had to dig pits in the sand to shelter from the bitterly cold night wind.

Day 4. Despite being close to death, Saint-Exupéry and Prévot struggled on.

In their final hours, they had a stroke of luck. The pair spotted a camp of local Bedouin tribesmen, and were saved.

Restless skies

Howling storms known as *hurricanes* usually form over warm oceans, but often spread onto coastlands. The strongest bring lashing rain and winds of over 250km/h (155mph), that can devastate entire towns.

Storm warnings

- Dark, green or black sky
- Hailstones
- Low, fast-moving clouds
- Roaring sounds in the air

Going underground

People who live in storm-risk areas often build a *storm shelter* in the ground near their home.

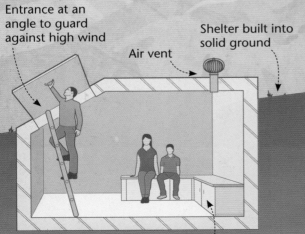

Entrance at an angle to guard against high wind

Air vent

Shelter built into solid ground

Food and water for two days

Lightning crashes to the ground as a supercell thunderstorm gathers over central Kansas, USA.

Lightning safety

- Take shelter inside a car or building
- Never shelter under trees or high objects – these attract lightning strikes
- Lie in a ditch, or close to the ground, if caught in the open

Lightning storms

In some parts of the world, especially the USA, thunderstorms can gather into vast clouds called *supercells*. These often generate bolts of lightning and golfball-sized hailstones, and can whip up violent winds called *tornadoes*.

Animal hazard: polar bears

- **Main distribution:** all across the Arctic
- **Max. length:** 3m (10ft)
- **Speed on land:** 40km/h (25mph)
- **Speed in water:** 10km/h (6mph)
- **Death toll on humans:** less than 1 per year

Survival zone:
Snow and ice

Icy, mountainous and streaked by hidden cracks called *crevasses*, the frozen parts of the world are a true test of endurance for climbers and explorers.

North

The North Pole is found on the frozen surface of the seas between Russia and North America.

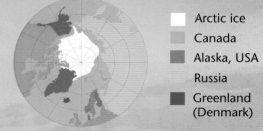

- Arctic ice
- Canada
- Alaska, USA
- Russia
- Greenland (Denmark)

South

The South Pole lies within the continent of Antarctica – an area of land twice the size of Australia. It's covered in ice sheets called *glaciers* all year round.

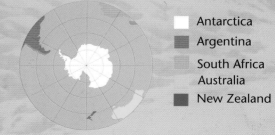

- Antarctica
- Argentina
- South Africa
- Australia
- New Zealand

23

Death from above

Snow-capped mountains may look peaceful and safe, but they can unleash deadly *avalanches* — fast-moving snowfalls that can knock people off ledges or bury them beneath mounds of snow.

Safety on ice

Mountain explorers always travel in teams roped together. If one team member falls into a crevasse or is caught in a snow drift, the others can provide instant aid.

Team leader

Each team member is connected to another by a rope.

Avoiding an avalanche

Stay away from narrow valleys when there has been recent, heavy snowfall that may get dislodged.

Surviving an avalanche

- Keep your nose and mouth covered.
- Lie on your back and slide with the flow, instead of rolling into a ball.

Using an ice tool to test the ground in front

The rest of the team tread in the footsteps of the leader.

Crossing a crevasse on the way to the top of Mount Everest, Nepal

Swallowed alive

Glaciers hold a deadly trap for hikers – deep crevasses that are often hidden by a layer of soft snow.

Surviving a fall

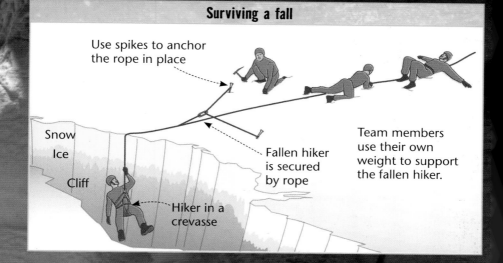

Use spikes to anchor the rope in place

Snow

Ice

Cliff

Hiker in a crevasse

Fallen hiker is secured by rope

Team members use their own weight to support the fallen hiker.

Getting out of the wind

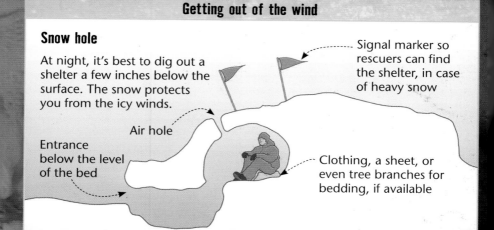

Snow hole

At night, it's best to dig out a shelter a few inches below the surface. The snow protects you from the icy winds.

Signal marker so rescuers can find the shelter, in case of heavy snow

Air hole

Entrance below the level of the bed

Clothing, a sheet, or even tree branches for bedding, if available

Trapped in the ice

DATE: January, 1915

LOCATION: The Weddell Sea, northwest of Antarctica

BACKGROUND: Anglo-Irish explorer Ernest Shackleton and 27 men sail on the ship *Endurance*. Their mission: to be the first team to cross the continent of Antarctica.

ARGENTINA

South Georgia

Elephant Island

Weddell Sea

ANTARCTICA

Disaster strikes

By late January (summer in Antarctica), *Endurance* was caught in a huge plain of freezing sea ice.

Endurance

For ten months, the ship drifted north with the ice pack. In October 1915, the ship began to collapse.

Shackleton and his men dragged three lifeboats – and their dwindling supplies – onto the ice to make camp.

Shackleton

The ice sheet finally thawed and cracked apart in April 1916. The crew managed to sail 160km (100 miles) to Elephant Island.

Shackleton knew that he and his crew were unlikely to be rescued from this remote, uninhabited island. So he decided to split the party in two.

One group huddled for shelter underneath two of the lifeboats...

...while Shackleton and five men rowed and sailed in the other boat for 17 days, across treacherous, raging seas...

Once on the island, the team still had to trek for 36 hours to cross snowy mountains, glaciers and sheer cliffs before they found help.

...to reach the inhabited island of South Georgia.

Shackleton arrived on South Georgia on May 16th. It took him three attempts to return to Elephant Island, because the pack ice was so thick.

◄----The *Yelcho*

The rest of the team were finally rescued by the tug steamer *Yelcho* in August 1916, after surviving in an icy wasteland for a total of 20 months.

Hard to reach

With jagged peaks, few tracks or roads and extreme cold, mountains can be full of dangers. Rescuers need the right tools and training to save people on the slopes.

An Alpine mountain rescue team fly in to assist an injured skier.

Frost-resistant rotors protect the helicopter from extreme cold.

Pilots receive special training to fly in dangerous fog and icy weather.

Tail skid stops the tail rotor from hitting rocks or cliffs.

Skis allow for a smooth landing on snowy ground.

Winch, cable and harness to reach people in awkward locations

A team will try to hike to the rescue point before the helicopter arrives, to offer first aid and prepare a landing spot.

Off—road rescue vehicles

Rescue teams use a fleet of off-road machines to reach injured climbers.

Sled

Stretcher

Subaru Forester
(US Mountain rescue, 1990—present)

High-powered lights on the roof, as well as headlights

Winch for pulling vehicles that are trapped in snow

Body of car sits 38cm (15in) above the ground.

Wheels designed not to get stuck in mud or snow

Tracked vehicles can cross the thickest snow and ice.

Kassbohrer All—Terrain Vehicle (ATV)
(Scotland, 1990—present)

MOUNTAIN RESCUE

Enclosed cabin to provide basic first aid and gently warm frozen people

Caterpillar tracks to cross slippery and rough ground

Surviving the cold

Freezing weather, high winds and cold water make the human body lose heat quickly. Survivors need the right shelter and skills to stay warm.

Snowbound

If a car gets stuck in a remote place, it is safest to stay inside and wait for rescue.

Before driving in the snow

- Check that the car is in good working order.
- Make sure someone has a telephone.
- Pack a blanket and a flashlight.

Run the engine to stay warm, but only for 10 minutes every hour, to conserve fuel.

Attach a bright object somewhere visible.

When the engine is on, turn the wheels from side to side to keep the path clear.

Leave a window open for ventilation, at least a handwidth.

Clear snow off the roof, and keep the exhaust pipe clear.

Icy water

If you tread on ice that is less than 5cm (2in) thick, you're likely to fall through into the freezing water below.

Water temperature:	Survival time:
0-4.5°C (32-40°F)	less than 15 minutes
4.5-10°C (40-50°F)	up to an hour
10-15.5°C (50-60°F)	around 6 hours
15.5-21°C (60-70°F)	around 12 hours
21°C (70°F) and up	several days

1. Don't panic

Falling into ice water is a real shock. Try to control breathing and stay afloat.

2. Stay where you are

Start climbing out at the spot where you fell in – don't try to make a new hole.

3. Climb out

Kick down with your legs to help push your body out of the water, and drag yourself back onto the ice.

4. Don't stand up

Roll away from the hole. Spreading your weight reduces the pressure on the ice.

5. Get warm

• Roll in the snow, which absorbs cold water, then remove wet clothes.
• Get to shelter and blankets.
• Drink warm liquids.

Driving into danger

Journeys that turn off the beaten track
can lead to sticky situations.

Crossing a river

Most cars can cope with water, as long as it
doesn't get into the engine. Walk the crossing
first, to check it's not too deep.

Adventurous
drivers can compete
in *off-road* races,
covering deserts, hill
country and the
wilderness.

Turn off the lights, unlock all
doors and open all windows.

Always cross downstream, so
the flow of water can help push
the car out on the far side.

This off-road car is
equipped with a snorkel,
allowing air into and out
of the engine.

Don't slow
down in the
water; keep
on moving.

Underwater

If a car is plunging into a river or lake, the best thing to do is get out of the car as quickly as possible.

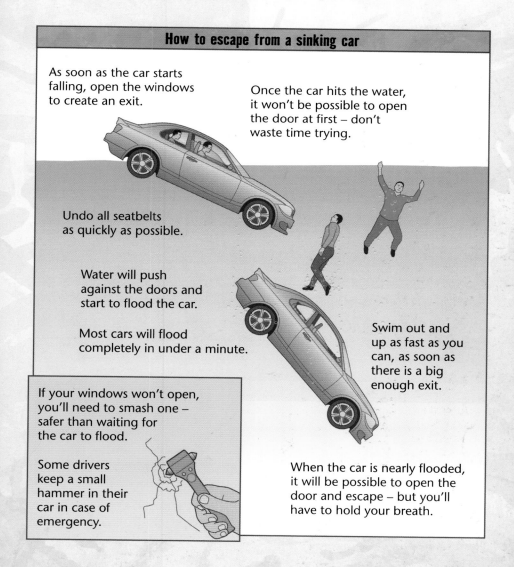

How to escape from a sinking car

As soon as the car starts falling, open the windows to create an exit.

Once the car hits the water, it won't be possible to open the door at first – don't waste time trying.

Undo all seatbelts as quickly as possible.

Water will push against the doors and start to flood the car.

Most cars will flood completely in under a minute.

Swim out and up as fast as you can, as soon as there is a big enough exit.

If your windows won't open, you'll need to smash one – safer than waiting for the car to flood.

Some drivers keep a small hammer in their car in case of emergency.

When the car is nearly flooded, it will be possible to open the door and escape – but you'll have to hold your breath.

Dangers of the woods

- Getting lost
- Exposure
- Injury: uneven terrain can cause trips, falls and broken bones.
- Animal hazards: bears, wolves, wild boar and even deer may attack if a person comes too close.

Survival zone:
Temperate forest

The Earth's *temperate* zones lie between the steamy tropics and icy poles. Forests and mountains are crisscrossed by fast-flowing rivers, and are home to many large animals.

A blanket of fog makes it even easier to get lost in the woods.

Animal hazard: bears

There are two types of bears in woodland areas: *brown bears*, also called *grizzlies*, and *black bears*.

Different types of bears can look similar. Being able to tell them apart could save your life...

Hump between shoulders

Small round ears

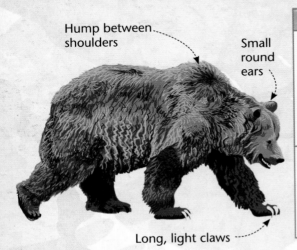

Long, light claws

Brown bear

- **Main distribution:** Alaska, Canada, northern Europe and Asia
- **Max. length:** 2.8m (9ft, 2in)
- **Death toll on humans:** around 5 per year.

- **Encountering a brown bear:**
  Curl into a ball and lie on the ground, pretending to be dead. With luck, the bear will simply wander off.

American black bear

- **Main distribution:** woodlands across North America
- **Max. length:** 2m (6ft, 6in)
- **Death toll on humans:** less than 1 per year.

- **Encountering a black bear:**
  1. Stand tall and wave arms in the air.
  2. Punch the bear in the nose or around the eyes.

Pointed ears

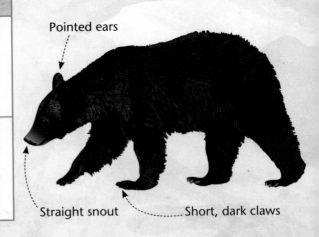

Straight snout

Short, dark claws

Survival challenge: crossing a river

Survival tip

Following a river or road is the surest method to find your way out of thick forests.

Avoid any deep or fast-flowing streches. Wide stretches are likely to be safer than narrow stretches.

Floating logs are a sign that the water is flowing too fast to cross.

Water tends to flow faster around islands – don't cross here.

Test the speed of the current by throwing a large stick into the water.

During the crossing

- Use a walking stick to test for depth, and to act as an extra support.
- Carry a backpack on one arm only, so it's easy to remove if you fall.
- Face upstream, so you can keep watch for any dangerous objects.
- Aim for a part of the bank that looks easy to climb onto.

Left for dead

DATE: August, 1823

LOCATION: The uncharted wilderness of South Dakota, USA

BACKGROUND: American fur trapper Hugh Glass is part of an expedition near the Missouri river. The group is exploring new territory, as well as looking for animal skins to sell.

Disaster strikes

Glass stumbled upon two bear cubs. Before he could creep away, their mother – a huge grizzly – loomed into view.

The bear raked Glass's body with her 15cm (6 inch) claws. Glass tried to fight back, but soon collapsed.

His companions found him unconscious, but still alive, and dragged him away.

Believing his injuries were fatal, they dug a shallow grave...

...and buried Glass in a bear-skin shroud.

Some days later, Glass woke up. He scratched his way out of the grave, only to find himself alone, and all his gear missing.

Scene of bear fight

Missouri river

Cheyenne river

Fort Kiowa

Unable to stand, he began to crawl, heading south to the Cheyenne river and civilization — 100 miles away.

Glass gradually built up his strength by eating roots and berries. In time, he was able to scare wolves off and eat their kills.

After six weeks of living off the land, Glass finally reached the Cheyenne, where he fashioned a raft from a fallen tree.

He paddled along the river to Fort Kiowa, where US government troops nursed him back to full health.

Glass went down in history as one of the greatest wilderness suriviors.

Deep adventure

People who explore the caverns and passages that stretch for miles below the Earth's surface are known as *cavers*. They follow safety rules to help them survive in this dark underworld.

Going in

- Never go caving alone. Groups of four or five cavers are safest.
- Always tell someone where you are going, and the time you expect to return.
- Pack a heat blanket and high energy snacks in case you get trapped.

Staying safe

- Leave arrows made of pebbles to show the way you've come.
- Carry a whistle to attract attention.
- If someone has an accident, send two people back to find help – but don't leave the injured person on their own.

A team of cavers climb 70m (277ft) to escape Green's Well in Alabama, USA.

Caving kit

Helmet

Light

Mountaineering equipment for climbing up and down steep caves

Overalls to keep the damp out

Knee pads

Elbow pads

Water bottle

Always carry back-up lights.

Strong boots

Survival zone:
Tropical rainforest

Biting insects, heavy rains and burning heat make the tropical zones of our world tough places to survive.

The tropical zone, or *tropics*, lies south of the Tropic of Cancer, and north of the Tropic of Capricorn.

Tropic of
Cancer

Tropic of
Capricorn

Rainforests

Tropical zones are often covered in dense forest known as *jungle* or *rainforest*.

Sekumpul Waterfalls, northern jungles of Bali, Indonesia

Jungle shelter

Even in the warmth of the jungle, a good shelter is essential. It will keep you dry and can protect you from insects and large animals, too.

Build an elevated platform using branches or conveniently-located trees.

Make a shelter to lean over the platform. Cover it with evergreen leaves to keep rain off.

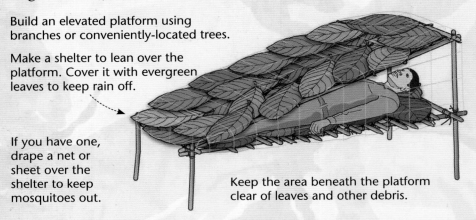

If you have one, drape a net or sheet over the shelter to keep mosquitoes out.

Keep the area beneath the platform clear of leaves and other debris.

Survival tip: making cordage

Jungles are filled with vines and large fronds, both useful for making string or rope, known generally as *cordage*.

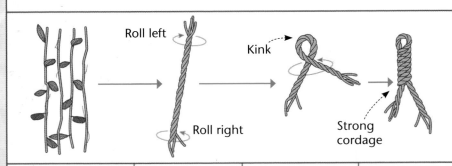

Roll left

Roll right

Kink

Strong cordage

1. Find lengths of leaves, thin roots, or bark. Split each one into a set of long, thin strips.	2. Take a bundle of three to six strips and roll them together.	3. Eventually, a kink will form, and the strand will bend into two halves.	4. Keep rolling, and the two halves will twist around each other.

Reading the land

It's possible to find useful tools and even to find a way out of a jungle without needing any equipment.

Follow downward slopes, which may well lead to water, or even a river.

Build shelters away from animal tracks and areas that could flood.

Survival tip

Break branches at eye level to leave a trail for yourself and any rescuers.

Most rivers eventually lead to settlements and allow a clear route out of the jungle.

Follow large animal trails, which will probably lead to a clearing or a river – but steer clear of the animal itself.

Hidden dangers

The greatest dangers of any jungle come from the creatures that live in it, especially some of the very smallest.

Anopheles mosquito

- **Main distribution:** sub-Saharan Africa
- **Diseases carried:** malaria, dengue fever, West Nile virus
- **Death toll on humans:** over 1 million per year
- **Max. size:** 16mm (0.7in)

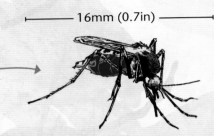

16mm (0.7in)

Most mosquito bites are harmless, but the female *anopheles* mosquito is one of the deadliest creatures on Earth.

50mm (2in)

Wide, orange head

Asian hornets release venom with each sting. Anyone stung repeatedly is at risk of kidney failure and death.

Asian giant hornet

- **Main distribution:** forests and jungles of East Asia
- **Max. size:** body 50mm (2in); stinger 6mm (0.25in)
- **Death toll on humans:** over 100 per year

Bullet ant

- **Main distribution:** rainforests of Central and South America
- **Nest locations:** around the base of trees; ants explore up trunks rather than along the ground
- **Max. size:** 30mm (1.2in)

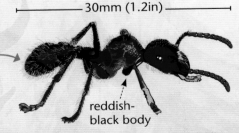

30mm (1.2in)

reddish-black body

Although not fatal, the sting of a bullet ant causes extreme pain and temporary paralysis around the area for 24 hours.

Bothrops pitvipers have flat snouts.

Pitvipers all have small pits close to their eyes.

Bothrops Lanceolatus, also called the *fer-de-lance*, produces venom that can cause prolonged bleeding, and can be fatal without rapid medical treatment.

Bothrops pitviper

- **Main distribution:** Central America and islands in the Caribbean
- **Body length:** 50cm-200cm (20in-6ft 6in)
- **Death toll on humans:** over 1,000 per year.

Jungle survivor

DATE: December, 1971

LOCATION: Peruvian rainforest

BACKGROUND: Juliane Koepcke, a German-Peruvian student, was flying with her mother from Lima to the jungle town Pucallpa, to meet her father.

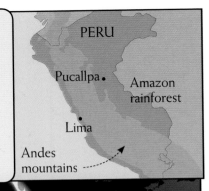

PERU

Pucallpa•

Amazon rainforest

•Lima

Andes mountains

Disaster strikes

Approaching a chain of mountains, the plane flew into a thunderstorm.

A bolt of lightning struck the plane, igniting the fuel tanks and ripping a wing off the body of the plane.

Strapped into a row of seats, Koepcke fell two miles through the sky...

...before crashing into the forest canopy. The thick jungle vines slowed her perilous descent.

Koepcke woke up lying under the row of seats. She had survived the fall, albeit with a broken collar bone, severe cuts and a black eye.

She stumbled through scattered plane debris, but found no other passengers.

She did discover a bag of hard candy, that would be her only food for the next week and a half.

Koepcke had learned some tips on jungle survival from her father. She started by finding a stream...

...then followed its course, hoping it would lead to a settlement.

After nine days of wading, and carefully avoiding alligators, snakes and piranha fish, she found a motor boat and a shelter.

Following another tip from her father, Koepcke used the fuel from the motor...

...to wash out her cuts, which had become infested with worms.

Two days later, local men found her and took her to the nearest town in a canoe. Koepcke emerged as the only survivor of Flight 508 from Lima.

House on fire

House fires produce toxic smoke and deadly heat.
The best advice is to get out of the house as quickly
as possible, and then call for help.

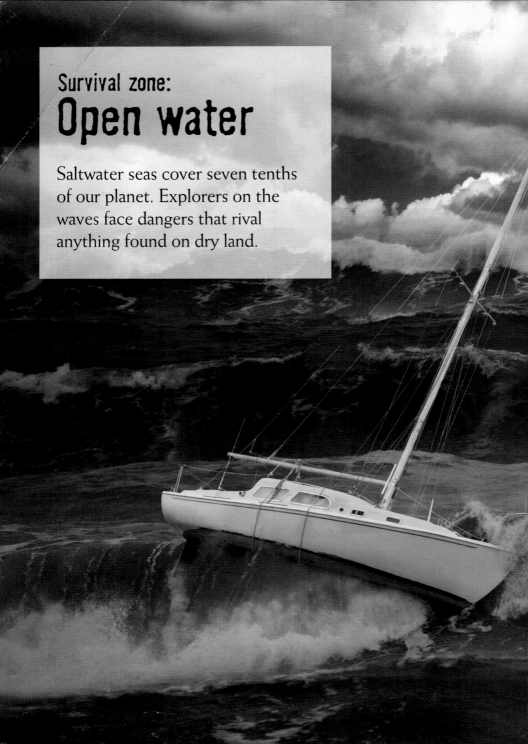

Survival zone:
Open water

Saltwater seas cover seven tenths of our planet. Explorers on the waves face dangers that rival anything found on dry land.

Sailing hazards

- **Typhoon**: tropical storms that can spring up rapidly, with winds strong enough to rip away sails.
- **Tsunami**: gigantic waves caused by tremors on the ocean floor.
- **Rogue** or **freak waves**: rarely occuring and unpredictable waves that rise incredibly high – sometimes high enough to overturn vast container ships.
- **Rocks** and **reefs**: In coastal waters, rocks hidden just below the surface can strike hulls without warning.
- **Icebergs**: massive blocks of ice that float in cold waters, often shrouded in sea fog.

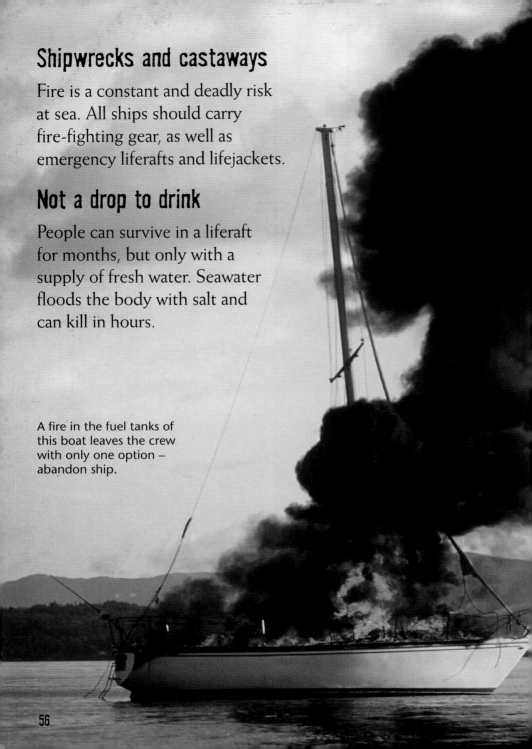

Shipwrecks and castaways

Fire is a constant and deadly risk at sea. All ships should carry fire-fighting gear, as well as emergency liferafts and lifejackets.

Not a drop to drink

People can survive in a liferaft for months, but only with a supply of fresh water. Seawater floods the body with salt and can kill in hours.

A fire in the fuel tanks of this boat leaves the crew with only one option – abandon ship.

275N lifejacket (designed for extreme conditions)

Lifejackets are essential deep water survival kit. They use gas canisters to self-inflate and will keep a person upright and afloat, even in savage seas.

Whistle to attract attention

Fully inflated gas canisters in here

Reflective strips

SeaGo offshore liferaft (can hold 4 to 6 people)

Canopy to guard against sun and rain

Solar still, to distill fresh water from seawater

Ladder to help people climb in

Fins to stabilize the raft

How a solar still works

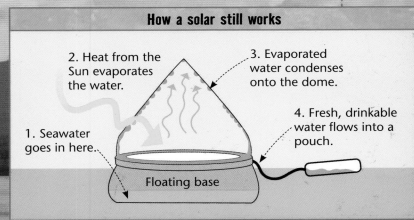

2. Heat from the Sun evaporates the water.

3. Evaporated water condenses onto the dome.

1. Seawater goes in here.

4. Fresh, drinkable water flows into a pouch.

Floating base

Dangers of the deep

Few sea creatures will hunt humans as food, but if a castaway is bleeding and splashing in the water, it could attract a killer shark.

Most attacks happen when a shark mistakes a swimmer for a seal. The deadliest species are *tiger sharks*, *bull sharks* and *great white sharks*.

A great white can smell traces of blood on ocean currents from up to 3km (2 miles) away.

Great white shark

- **Main distribution:** temperate waters all around the world
- **Max. length:** 6m (20ft)
- **Death toll on humans:** around 1 per year

Young tiger sharks have a visible stripe pattern across their backs.

Tiger shark

- **Main distribution:** tropical waters in the central Pacific Ocean
- **Max. length:** 5m (16ft)
- **Death toll on humans:** around 1 per year

An attacking shark can be scared off by a punch to the eyes, gills and snout.

Don't swim alone! Sharks are are less likely to attack a group of people in the water than a lone swimmer.

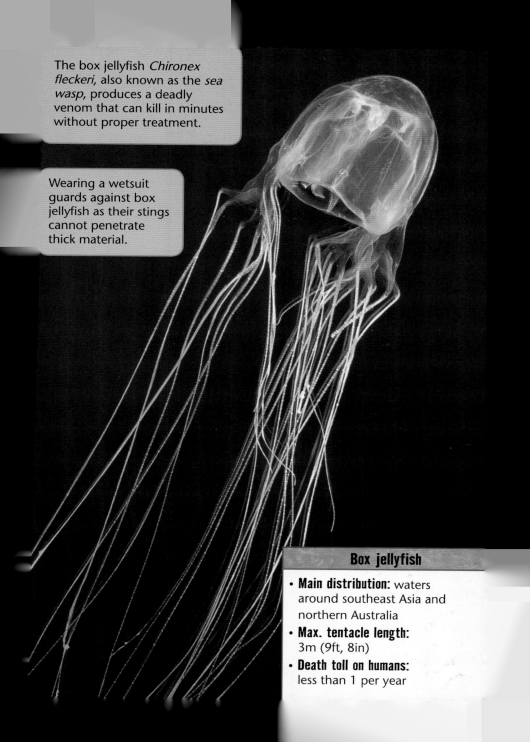

The box jellyfish *Chironex fleckeri*, also known as the *sea wasp*, produces a deadly venom that can kill in minutes without proper treatment.

Wearing a wetsuit guards against box jellyfish as their stings cannot penetrate thick material.

Box jellyfish

- **Main distribution:** waters around southeast Asia and northern Australia
- **Max. tentacle length:** 3m (9ft, 8in)
- **Death toll on humans:** less than 1 per year

Lost at sea

DATE: March, 1973

LOCATION: The Pacific Ocean, near Central America

BACKGROUND: Maurice and Maralyn Bailey had set sail from Panama to the Galapagos Islands on their 31ft (9.4m) sailing yacht, *Auralyn*. The journey was expected to last for about two weeks.

Disaster strikes

Just after dawn one morning, Maralyn felt the yacht strike something. She looked overboard, to see an injured sperm whale thrashing around in a pool of blood.

The whale had collided with the yacht, making a large hole. The *Auralyn* began to sink...

Avon   *Avon II*

The Baileys threw some supplies into their emergency liferafts, both named *Avon*, and roped them together.

Making hooks from safety pins, they caught fish and small turtles to eat.

They collected drinking water from rain and dew that settled on the raft canopy.

Over the next three months, they spotted seven passing ships, and used flares to attract attention...

...with no luck.

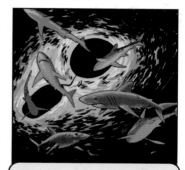

One day, a school of sharks gathered beneath the rafts.

The Baileys managed to catch and eat the smaller ones, and eventually the school moved on.

Finally, after 117 days adrift, they were rescued by a Korean fishing boat.

Life savers

Rescuers use special vehicles and search equipment to find and save anyone lost at sea.

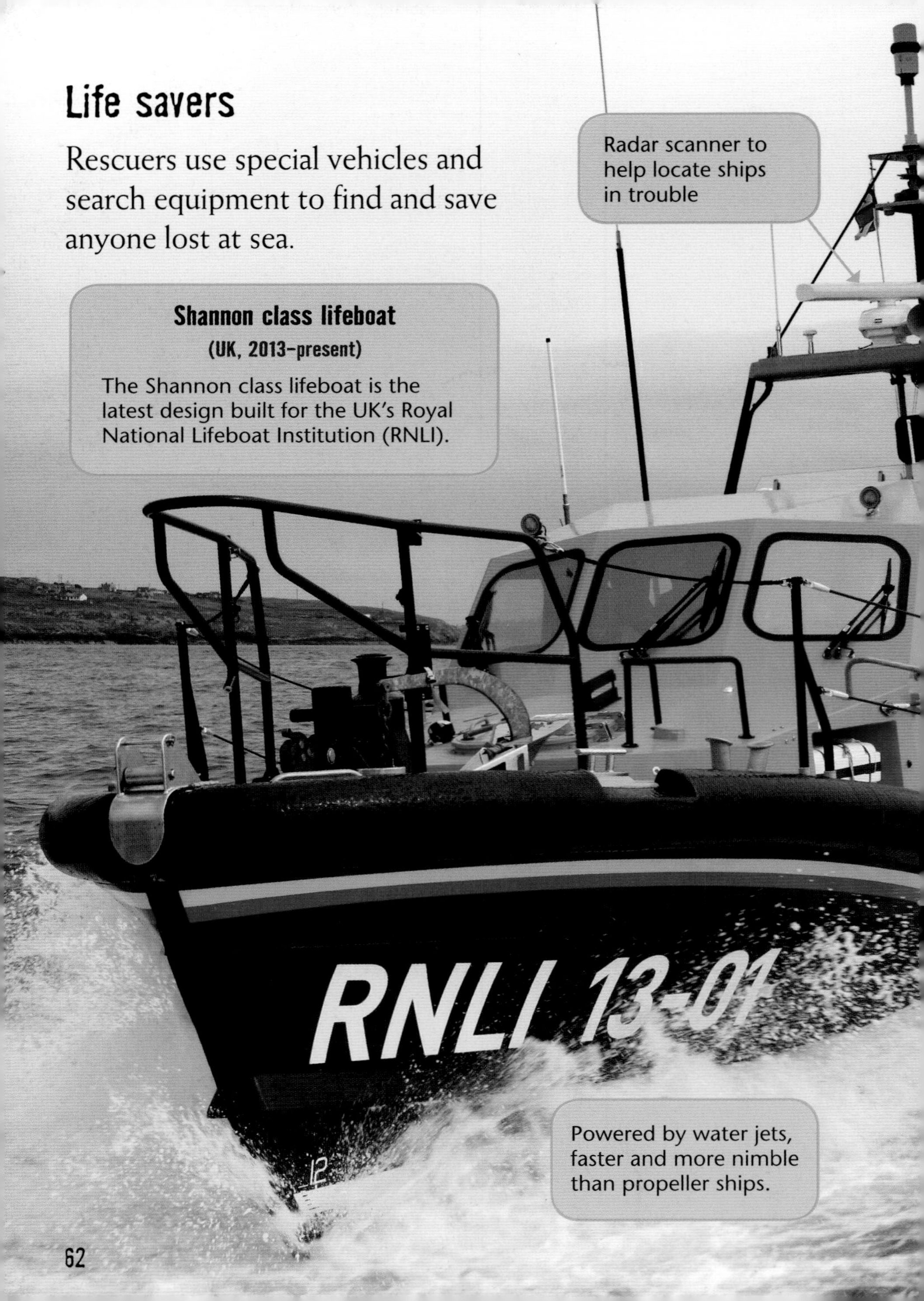

Radar scanner to help locate ships in trouble

Shannon class lifeboat

(UK, 2013–present)

The Shannon class lifeboat is the latest design built for the UK's Royal National Lifeboat Institution (RNLI).

RNLI 13-01

Powered by water jets, faster and more nimble than propeller ships.

Space for two six-person liferafts

Air rescue

AgustaWestland AW139 helicopter
(Used worldwide, 2003–present)

Onboard computers allow the helicopter to hover in position while the crew operates the winch.

Winch inside here

Powerful radar scanner and infrared search equipment located in the nose

Radio rescue

Most small ships carry emergency radio beacons that fix their location when disaster strikes.

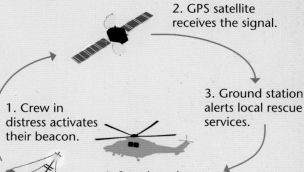

2. GPS satellite receives the signal.

3. Ground station alerts local rescue services.

1. Crew in distress activates their beacon.

4. Search and rescue begins.

Crash landings

If a helicopter crashes over water, the crew has seconds to escape. Helicopter rescue teams, and people who fly to offshore sites such as oil platforms, have to undergo training in a simulator.

An oil platform worker takes a HUET course: Helicopter Underwater Escape *or* Egress Training at a facility in Aberdeen, Scotland.

HUET basics

1. Brace for impact

A mechanical arm lowers the training tank into a pool. The crew members each look for the nearest escape point and mark it with one hand.

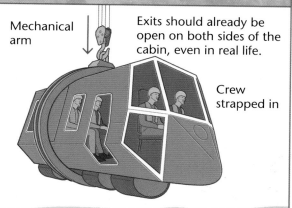

Mechanical arm

Exits should already be open on both sides of the cabin, even in real life.

Crew strapped in

2. Getting your bearings

It's likely that the helicopter will turn over or flip in one direction or another. The crew waits for it to stop rolling, then release their straps.

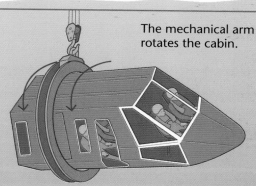

The mechanical arm rotates the cabin.

3. Escape

The crew use their marker points to guide themselves out of the cabin. Inflating their lifejackets will help push each one up to the surface.

A helicopter is unlikely to sink very deep in real life.

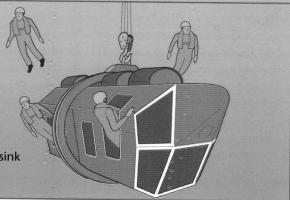

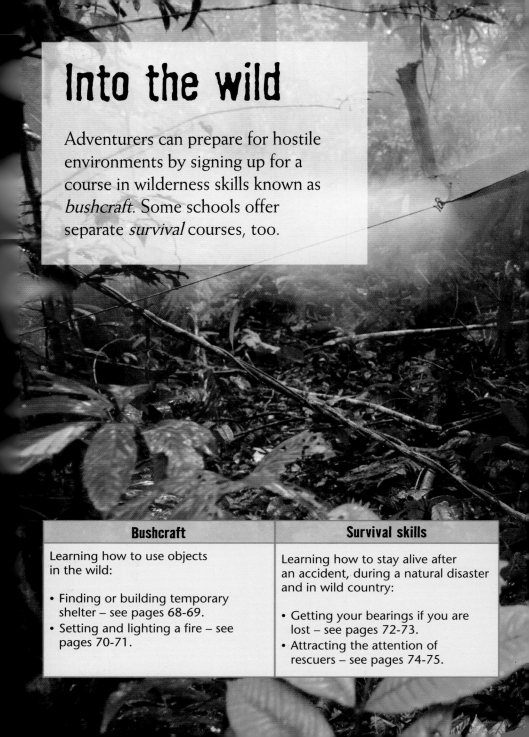

Into the wild

Adventurers can prepare for hostile environments by signing up for a course in wilderness skills known as *bushcraft*. Some schools offer separate *survival* courses, too.

Bushcraft	Survival skills
Learning how to use objects in the wild:	Learning how to stay alive after an accident, during a natural disaster and in wild country:
• Finding or building temporary shelter – see pages 68-69. • Setting and lighting a fire – see pages 70-71.	• Getting your bearings if you are lost – see pages 72-73. • Attracting the attention of rescuers – see pages 74-75.

A survival expert is getting a fire going at his camp in the Amazon Rainforest. The oxygen from his breath helps the flames to grow.

A night in the wild

Most survival training includes spending a night alone in rough country. Some simple survival skills can help anyone stay safe if they find themselves alone in the wilderness.

Finding shelter

Exposure to the cold, especially at night, can be fatal. The first priority is to find a safe place to shelter.

1. Caves

- The back of a small cave is likely to be warm and dry.
- Look for tracks, discarded bones and other signs of animal life, to check that the cave is unoccupied.

2. Rocky overhang

- Even a rocky outcrop or boulder can provide useful shelter.
- Always check that the walls above are solid and dry.

3. Fallen trees

- Lean branches against the tree trunk and seal any gaps with leaves, moss and clumps of earth.

Survival challenge: build a shelter

If there are no safe natural shelters nearby, it's usually possible to build a temporary shelter for the night.

Always leave a marker or sign, such as a bright flag, to show where you are.

An outer layer of leaves and moss keeps the shelter dry and warm.

Thick branches make a frame.

Try to weave smaller sticks together on each side.

A simple platform made from branches can keep you away from damp ground.

Firecraft

A small fire provides heat and light and can be used to cook food, to dry out wet clothes and warn away wild animals.

Preparing a fire
1. Clear a space - at least 1m (3ft) on all sides, to make sure the fire cannot spread
2. Gather materials To make a fire, you will need *tinder*, *kindling* and *fuel*.
3. Keep it dry Build a platform of twigs to hold the fire off damp ground.

- **Tinder**: something very dry that will catch fire easily, such as bark shavings, dandelion fluff or straw.

- **Kindling**: very thin, very dry sticks that will light quickly when exposed to a flame.

- **Fuel**: logs or branches. Fuel will take several minutes to catch fire, but should burn for a long time.

4. Strike a light

Lighting a fire requires an *igniter*, such as a match. Many survival experts prefer to carry a *fire rod and striker*, as matches run out, and can get damp.

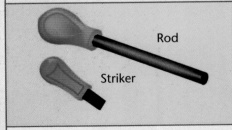

Scraping the striker along the rod produces very hot sparks.

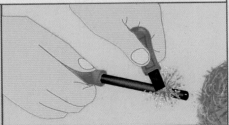

As the shower of sparks reaches the tinder, it should immediately catch fire.

Survival challenge: build a tepee fire

Tepee fires generate lots of heat, and send fire high up to act as a clear beacon.

Clear the ground around the base of the fire.

Use large sticks to build up a pyramid-shaped wall. Add more sticks to keep the fire going.

Leave an opening in the wall so the igniter can reach the tinder and kindling inside.

Finding your way home

Getting a sense of your location and direction will help you move towards safety and possible rescue.

Solar power

As long as the Sun is visible, it's possible to work out which way is north.

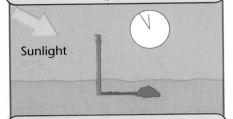

1. Just before midday, find a clear patch of land and push a straight stick into the ground.

Sunlight

The Sun always rises in the east and sets in the west. This means it's easy to identify which direction you are facing.

2. Place a rock at the end of the stick's shadow.

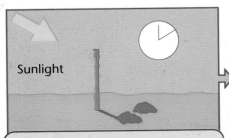

Sunlight

Sunlight

3. Wait for 15 minutes. The shadow will move – place a second rock where the shadow ends up.

4. Put your left foot on the first rock, and your right foot on the second rock, facing away from the Sun. You are now facing north.

Using the stars

Over the course of a night, the stars appear to move across the sky. In the northern hemisphere, there is one star, known as the *north star*, that doesn't move much. As you look up to see it, it is always to the north.

This photograph shows the location of the north star. Other stars appear to circle around it during the night; in fact, it's the Earth that spins.

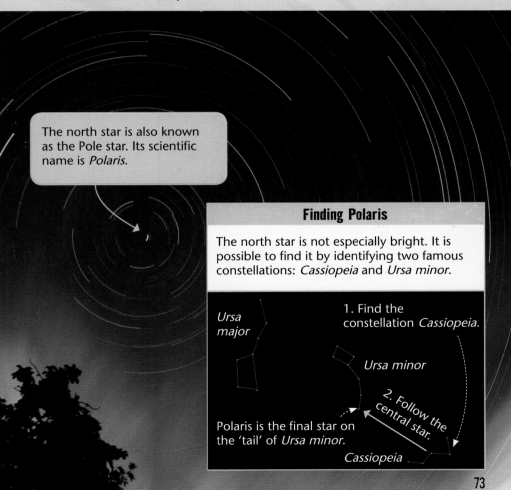

The north star is also known as the Pole star. Its scientific name is *Polaris*.

Finding Polaris

The north star is not especially bright. It is possible to find it by identifying two famous constellations: *Cassiopeia* and *Ursa minor*.

Ursa major

1. Find the constellation *Cassiopeia*.

Ursa minor

2. Follow the central star.

Polaris is the final star on the 'tail' of *Ursa minor*.

Cassiopeia

Getting noticed

Survivors can attract the attention of rescue teams by using signals or emergency messages that are recognized around the world.

Mark out a giant message on the ground

Use clothes or objects around you, such as rocks or piles of leaves, to create a signal visible to passing aircraft.

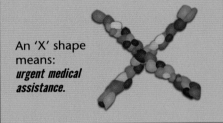

An 'X' shape means: *urgent medical assistance.*

A 'V' shape means: *require assistance.*

Shine sunlight off a mirror

The flash from a mirror or shiny object can be visible to people over 30km (20 miles) distant. Shining a light onto a ship in a repeating pattern acts as a beacon.

1. Make a 'V' with your fingers, and hold it up so the ship is between them.

2. Tilt the mirror until a dot of sunlight shines onto your hand.

3. Lift the mirror so the dot shines between your fingers, and onto the ship.

4. Move the mirror back and forth, to make this light appear to flash.

Build a signal fire

Smoke trails can be spotted by passing ships or aircraft.

Cover the fire with fresh branches.

Keep an opening just above the fire.

Platform

Construct a platform from large branches, and light a dry fire inside it. Find out how to set up a fire on page 70.

Only light the fire when a vehicle comes within eye or earshot.

Body language

If you're in open ground, you can signal to rescue aircraft using your body.

Standing straight with both arms raised means: *pick us up*.

Bending your legs, with your arms pointing in one direction means: *land here*.

Miracle survivors

Accidents can happen at any time, with no one to blame. Surviving a freak accident is often a matter of luck.

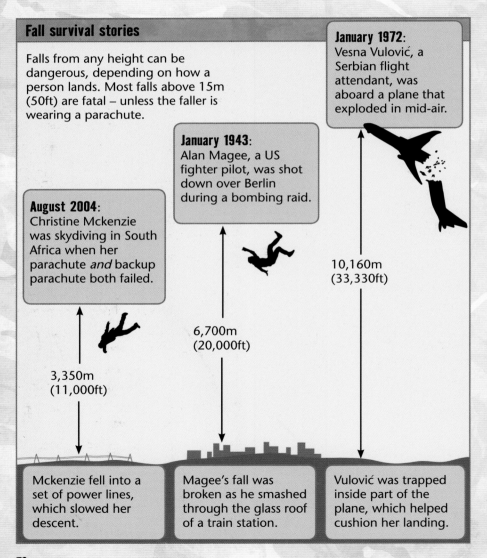

Fall survival stories

Falls from any height can be dangerous, depending on how a person lands. Most falls above 15m (50ft) are fatal – unless the faller is wearing a parachute.

January 1972: Vesna Vulović, a Serbian flight attendant, was aboard a plane that exploded in mid-air.

January 1943: Alan Magee, a US fighter pilot, was shot down over Berlin during a bombing raid.

August 2004: Christine Mckenzie was skydiving in South Africa when her parachute *and* backup parachute both failed.

10,160m (33,330ft)

6,700m (20,000ft)

3,350m (11,000ft)

Mckenzie fell into a set of power lines, which slowed her descent.

Magee's fall was broken as he smashed through the glass roof of a train station.

Vulović was trapped inside part of the plane, which helped cushion her landing.

Glossary

This glossary explains some of the words used in this book.
If a word is written in *italic* type, it has an entry of its own.

Antarctic The region around the South Pole.

Arctic The region around the North Pole.

ATV All-Terrain Vehicle, often used to reach injured climbers and hikers in wild country.

avalanche A sudden rush of unstable mountain snow.

beacon A small device that sends a pulse of light or radio waves to searching rescuers.

bushcraft Information and skills that help someone to survive outdoors.

caver Someone who explores underground caverns.

cordage Rope or string made from materials found in the wild.

crampons Sharp spikes that clip to climbing boots and provide a solid grip on ice and snow.

crevasse A deep crack or break in a *glacier*.

debris shelter A simple shelter made from branches, leaves and moss.

desert An area that receives little or no rainfall for most of the year.

dew trap Plastic or cloth sheeting that catches drips of water from the air.

flare A capsule that releases a steady stream of smoke, used as a distress signal.

glacier A thick sheet of frozen ice.

grizzly Another name for North American brown bears.

hurricane A swirling storm accompanied by very strong, high speed winds.

kindling Small sticks and other materials that help a fire to grow.

machete A sharp, heavy knife useful for a range of survival tasks.

portaledge A canvas or plastic sleeping platform fixed to a rockface.

rainforest A warm, wet forest, usually filled with plants and animals.

snorkel A tube that keeps a flow of air open to a submerged engine or person.

snow hole A small, dug-out shelter under the surface of the snow.

solar still A device to collect freshwater from the air using heat from the Sun.

storm shelter An underground hiding place from violent weather.

temperate zone The regions between the *tropics* and the poles.

tinder Very dry material that catches fire easily.

tropics The hot regions of the Earth close to the equator.

Index

Acknowledgements

Every effort has been made to trace and acknowledge ownership of copyright. If any rights have been omitted, the publishers offer to rectify this in any future editions following notification. The publishers are grateful to the following individuals and organizations for permission to reproduce material on the following pages:

cover Ice cave in a glacier in Westland Tai Poutini National Park © picturegarden / Getty images; **p1** Sidewinder rattlesnake, Arizona, USA © Don B. Stevenson / Alamy; **p2-3** © Carsten Peter / National Geographic / Getty images; **p4** © Jim Edds / Science Photo Library; **p5** © David Trood / Getty images; **p8** © David Trood / Getty images; **p11** © Ashley Cooper / Alamy; **p12-13** © National Geographic Image Collection / Alamy; **p14-15** © Steve Allen / Getty images; **p16-17** © Michael S. Lewis / National Geographic / Getty images; **p20-21** © Jim Reed / Science Faction / Getty images; **p22-23** Katmai National Park and Preserve © Paul Souders / Corbis; **p24-25** © Galen Rowell / Corbis; **p26-27** © National Geographic / Getty Images ; **p30-31** © François Pugnet / Kipa / Corbis; **p31** *vehicles* © Adrian Dean / F1ARTWORK; **p32-33** © Sverrir Thorolfsson Iceland / Getty images; **p34-35** © Henn Photography / Corbis; **p36-37** © 2013 Daniel Frauchiger / Getty images; **p42-43** © Stephen Alvarez / National Geographic / Getty images; **p44-45** © Stephen Alvarez / National Geographic / Getty images; **p49** © Martin Van Lokven / Foto Natura / Minden Pictures / Corbis; **p54-55** © John Lund / Corbis; **p56-57** © Chris Cheadle / Getty images; **p59** © Visual&Written SL / Alamy; **p62-63** © RNLI; **p63** *helicopter* © Adrian Dean / F1ARTWORK; **p64** © North Sea Oil / Alamy; **p66-67** © Pete McBride / National Geographic Image Collection / Alamy; **p69** © Benjamin Haas / Shutterstock; **p71** © Spaces Images / Alamy; **p73** © Malcolm Park astronomy images / Alamy.

Survival on the internet

For links to websites where you can learn more about survival skills, read true stories of miraculous escapes, and find out where you can go on a bushcraft traning course, go to the Usborne Quicklinks website at **www.usborne.com/quicklinks** and enter the keyword: **survival**.

Additional illustrations by Will Dawes, Anna Gould, Helen Edmonds, Amy Manning and Adrian Dean
Series editor: Jane Chisholm   Series designer: Zoe Wray
Digital design by John Russell   Picture research by Ruth King